STEPPIN' OVER THE GLASS:

LIFE JOURNEYS IN POETRY AND PROSE

JOHARI MAHASIN RASHAD

EVANSTON PUBLISHING, INC.
1216 HINMAN AVENUE
EVANSTON, IL 60202

in association with

Raw Ink Press
Washington, D.C.

Steppin' Over the Glass: Life Journeys in Poetry and Prose. ©Copyright 1992 by Johari Mahasin Rashad. All rights reserved. Printed in the United States of America. No part of this book may be used or reproduced in any manner whatsoever without written permission except in the case of brief quotations embodied in critical articles and reviews.

EVANSTON PUBLISHING, INC.
1216 HINMAN AVENUE
EVANSTON, IL 60202

This book is printed in association with
Raw Ink Press
P.O. Box 70417
Washington, D.C. 20024-0417

Photography by Anne Sanderoff-Walker

Excerpts from *The Dance of Anger* by Harriett Lerner. ©Copyright 1985 by Harriett Lerner.
Reprinted by permission of HarperCollins Publishers.

Excerpts from *The Language of Letting Go* by Melody Beattie.
©Copyright 1990 by Hazelden Foundation, Center City, Minnesota.
Reprinted by permission.

10 9 8 7 6 5 4 3 2 1

ISBN: 1-879260-05-0

DEDICATION

Life is partly what we make it, and partly what it is made by the friends whom we choose.

> -Tehyi Hsieh
> *Chinese Epigrams Inside Out and Proverbs*, 1948

For my friends: traveling companions who make life's journeys easier.

> Johari Mahasin Rashad
> Washington, D.C.
> January 1, 1992

OTHER BOOKS BY JOHARI MAHASIN RASHAD

(R)Evolutions, Writely So!, Washington, D.C. 1982.

A collection of poems which reflects one woman's life during a fifteen-year span from ages 15 to 30. These poems chronicle growth through experiences in college, the Women's Movement, the Civil Rights Movement, marriage, childbirth, and divorce.

Woman, too, Writely So!, Washington, D.C. 1984.

A collection of poetry focused on woman — not just the black woman, but the "everywoman" and her feelings and thoughts about men, her children, other women, her world, and herself. It is an affirmation of self and a celebration of things female.

JOHARI MAHASIN RASHAD

Johari Mahasin Rashad is a native of Washington, D.C. She received a B.A. in Afro-American Studies from Howard University and an M.A. in Adult Education/HRD from the University of the District of Columbia. She is studying for a Ph.D. in organizational communication at Howard University.

She started writing poetry in 1964 and has been a free-lance writer since 1974. Her poems, essays, books reviews, and articles have appeared in anthologies: (*The Afro-American Review; HOO-DOO 5, Special Women's Issue; SYNERGY: Anthology of DC Blackpoetry*); magazines (*Black Collegian; Women's Work; Class; Changing Woman Magazine; New Directions Magazine; OMOWE Journal*); and newspapers (*The Washington Post; The City Hall New Times; Managing Your Career*).

Her first book, *Federal Job-Hunting Simplified*, was published in 1979. Her books of poetry, *(R)Evolutions* and *Woman, too*, were published in 1982, and 1984, respectively. She was the Washington, D.C. correspondent for *Changing Woman Magazine* from 1986-1989.

Ms. Rashad has read and performed her poems on a variety of forums in the Washington metropolitan area since 1975. These include: the Ascension Poetry Series, the Martin Luther King Library Literary Friends Lunchtime Author Series, WPFW Radio's "The Poet and the Poem", and the Shakespeare Folger Library's Midday Muse Poetry Series. She produced and performed in a two-woman poetry show, "In Love and Trouble", at Howard University's Blackburn Center in November 1982. In the summer of 1985, several of her poems were performed in "By Word of Mouth", a performance play. Some of her poems appear in *Adam of Ife: Black Women in Praise of Black Men*, an poetry anthology edited by Naomi Long Madgett, published by Lotus Press (1992).

Ms. Rashad and her daughter, Chekesha, live in Washington, D.C.

TABLE OF CONTENTS

Foreword   1

Poems

Survival Steps	7
The Undressed Dancer	8
Even Up	9
The Woman in There	10
Erasable You	11
Mother's Day	12
Sisterlove #3	13
Steppin' Over the Glass	14
Changing Seasons	16
In Time...Unfinished	17
A Thief of Time	18
A Thanksgiving Prayer for All Souls	20
Fabricated Lady	21
A Stitch in Time	22
Station Break	23
Waiting Game	24
Be Loved	25
Sax Appeal	26
The Promised Land #3	27
Wake-Up Call	28
Plain Sight	29
It Takes All Kinds	31
Terminal Illness	33
Making the Grade	34
Building Blocks/Stepping Stones	35
A Parent's Prayer	36
Holding Patterns	38
Temporary In-Sad-ity	39
Memory Lapse	
(Unguarded Moments #2)	40
Beyond Control	41
Sitting This One Out	42

Woman Strength	43
A Measure of Time	45
Closed Doors/Open Windows	47

Prose

"Letting Go"
Meditation	51
Sermon	53
Benediction	61
Endnotes	63

FOREWORD

Have you ever stepped barefooted on a piece of glass? If so, you know what a painful (and bloody) experience that can be! Sometimes the glass gets embedded deep in our feet and requires major treatment to remove; other times, it just cuts the skin and the wound needs only peroxide and a band-aid. Either way, we get hurt, we cry, we bleed.

Daily life requires that we learn to step over the glass that is strewn across our pathways. "Glass" refers to the slings and arrows, the tears, the big and little hurts that are part of living. I was not raised on—and I've never lived on—clean, safe streets: there aren't any. Even when we keep our eyes clearly focused on the road ahead to ensure safe passage, we can't avoid getting hurt. Sometimes the piece of glass we step on causes only minor bleeding; sometimes it takes months or years for us to recover. Wouldn't it be great if we could avoid glass altogether?

We should expect to encounter glass (in the *lingua franca,* "shit happens") and to become adept at stepping over it. Even if we're nimble-footed, a piece of glass (a crisis or some other hurt) will get us sooner or later: it's inevitable.

A poem I wrote for my friend Diane Wood in 1987 inspired this book. I'm not an expert on coping with life's problems. While writing is a major means of catharsis for me, I know that with the help of friends, professionals, and solitude, stepping over glass is a skill that can be mastered. Best of all, my friends are ever-ready with hugs, band-aids, and lollipops.

My love and special thanks to: Jean Alexander, Sandra Anderson, Diane Armstrong, Ifama Arsan, Regina Beard, Dr. Michael Beasley, Leslie Botha, Olivia Bradshaw, Dolores (De) Burton, Florence Clark, Nathaniel Deutsch, Lloyd DeVore, Michael Durso, Anita and John Ford, George and Peggy Gluski, Fannie and David Hamilton, Bette Faye Hover,

Maret Hutchinson, Berner and Ray Ann Johnson, Bessie Johnson, Narvin Kimball, Ramona and Ken Litowsky, Margaret and James (Jay) McFadden, Lucy and Joel Petty, Anne Sanderoff-Walker, Annette Sturdevant, Joseph Torregano, Dr. Marciana Wilkerson, and the members of All Souls Unitarian Church.

POETRY

4
Steppin' over the Glass

I have three chairs in my house: one for solitude, two for friendship, three for company.
    -Henry David Thoreau

Solitude gives birth to the original in us, to beauty unfamiliar and perilous—to poetry...
   -Thomas Mann
   Death in Venice (1913)

It is so much easier to tell intimate things in the dark.
   -William McFee
   Casuals of the Sea (1916)

SURVIVAL STEPS

We walk around contradictions
tiptoe past inconsistencies
trying to survive

we ignore facts and figures
that stare at us
choke down hypocracies
in a mighty (un)conscious effort
to get through each day

Life can be so difficult
seeing things as they really are

sometimes you have to suspend
belief

just to get by.

(10/2/84)

THE UNDRESSED DANCER

The party's over
lights turned off
festive decorations torn down.

The undressed dancer
stands unnoticed
stripped of the shimmering
beads and glitter
that were hers for only a time.

The beautiful baubles
that once adorned
her now bare body
and caused her
to catch everyone's eyes
have been locked away.

The undressed dancer stands alone
her party partners are long gone—
it's rude to so quickly dismiss
a major party guest.

She stands there, waiting patiently:
the public that now so blithely
passes her by
will fall under her spell again.

(1/13/85)

EVEN UP

We talk to
at
around
each other
seldom on
the
same
level.

Our words
are serious
funny
intimate
but
not always
at
the
same
time.

Will we ever meet?

(10/13/85)

THE WOMAN IN THERE

(For Chekesha)

I've sometimes seen her—
the woman in there

she comes out occasionally.

You can tell by her stance
or the turn of her head

what an interesting woman
she's going to be!

(1986)

ERASABLE YOU

I wrote you down in pencil...
something told me
you had the air of temporary.

(12/19/86)

MOTHERS' DAY

Mother,

May the sun warm you today
May the breeze caress you
May all the flowers
turn their heads to you.

May you have a day
like you give others—
warm,
loving, and
beautiful.

(5/10/87)

SISTERLOVE #3

(For Ifama)

Oh, my sister,
though you have gone
your spirit still remains

your spirit
vibrant as crystal rainbows
sweet as lovers' kisses
welcome as summer rain

your spirit
lies scattered in bits and pieces
throughout the house
every place you touched

like lint on the living room carpet
dust motes in the air
crumbs on the kitchen counter
threads on the floor

I will collect all these pieces carefully
one by one
and store them
in a special place
where I'll return frequently
whenever I think of you.

(7/10/87)

STEPPIN' OVER THE GLASS

(For Diane)

Sister
I am not wiser than you
though it may sometimes seem
that I have all the answers.

My words to you
come not from books or movies
but from real-life lessons learned
by steppin' over the glass.

My problems and pains
are no fewer
or less painful
than your own

and while I may seem
to have it all together
I'm still learning the way.

I've come to where I am
through sharp-edged promises
broken relationships
shattered dreams—

knowledge like mine
is not without its costs;
my feet have been bloodied
by unseen shards
many times before.

So, my sister
I cannot lead you
I can only advise
by pointing out
the dangerous spots;

warning you
about sharp edges.

I've travelled this way for a while
I'll try to help you along
but I'm still learning, too,

to carefully step over the glass.

(12/31/87)

CHANGING SEASONS

It's time to button up again.

Winter came
cloaked in silence
bringing chills and ice
to a once-warm land.

The promises of spring
openness, light, new beginnings
grew to full blossom

under the sultry summer sun
and showed themselves proudly
to any who had eyes to see.

Fall brought changes
preparations for the cold;
the sun-drenched days of summer
faded slowly, sadly, away.

The cycle repeats itself
it's necessary to prepare
for the cold.
Spring always returns
but until then,
it's time to button up again.

(1/13/88)

IN TIME...UNFINISHED

In time
I'll learn to block the pain;
I've already put away your pictures
erased you from my appointment book
tried to put you out of my thoughts.

But you keep creeping back
at the oddest hours
our instant replays
seem beyond my control;
things we did and said
are not easily forgotten—
what I'd give for the ability
to rewind and erase!

In time
I'll no longer love you
but I'll remember you with affection.

(1/23/88)

A THIEF OF TIME

(For JT)

Seconds.
I live by seconds.
Clutching them greedily
spending them sparingly
Seconds.
I live by seconds...
I am a thief of time.

Minutes.
I gather minutes
trying futilely to keep them
from slipping through my fingers.
Minutes
I live by minutes...
I am a thief of time.

Hours.
When can I steal hours?
Hours are only wishes
hoped-for promises
mostly unfulfilled.

Days.
What I wouldn't give for days!
Not having to check my watch
ignoring clocks and calendars
not looking behind me.
I am not so good a thief
that I can steal days.

Seconds.
Minutes.
Hours.

I live by time.
I love you by the clock.
I need more time...

More time to work my magic
more time to drink my fill
more time
more time

Everyone who steals
wants something they
don't have...

In loving you,
I am a thief of time.

(8/11/88)

A THANKSGIVING PRAYER FOR ALL SOULS

(For All Souls Unitarian Church)

Our God

We thank you for this day, this place, these people.
We are grateful for this opportunity for us to be
together.

We thank you for the strength
to keep getting up when we've been pushed or
have fallen down;

We thank you for our small and large successes
and the experience we've gained from our failures;

We thank you for smiles and laughter
without which each day would be harder to bear;

We thank you for the ability to dream
and the power to make dreams come true;

We thank you for each chance you give us
to make a difference in this world.

Bless this food that we are about to eat
May it give us the strength
To face each new day unafraid
To raise our voices in the cause of justice
And to continue to make trouble when necessary.
Amen.

*(11/24/88: Written for the first ASC Thanksgiving
Community Dinner)*

FABRICATED LADY

I am a woman,
whole—
but of separate pieces
my flesh and bones
the warp and weft
my threads spun out

past me
past time
past distance.

The texture of my being
the result of many hands
human handiwork
disparate patches pieced together
creating the pattern of me....

a woman—whole.

I am cold
thin and see-through
vulnerable and transparent
delicate to the touch.

I am warm
wrap me around you,
wallow in me
feel my comfort and protection.

I am a tapestry
a quilt of many colors
reflecting carelessness,
slipped stitches, and
meticulous craftsmanship.

I am a woman,
whole—with no loose threads
a cloth of many pieces
with all seams intact.

(9/16/89)

A STITCH IN TIME

(Dedicated to the NAMES Project—the AIDS Quilt)

A stitch in time saves nine
a stitch in time saves lives
a stitch in time raises eyes
a stitch in time praises lives.

Common threads connect us,
stitches, in the fabric of time
pieces of many colors
bound together,
a multi-hued mosaic
proof positive
that love is universal.

From beginning to end,
each stitch interweaves with others
and the beauty of each life
does not stop
when the thread has been broken
or cut too short.

We will not forget.

Love, joy, and smiles remain
visible to all who remember...
each life, a unique thread, a stitch
which for a time,
embellished the fabric
of the Universe.

We will not forget.

A stitch in time saves nine...
a stitch in time savors lives...
a stitch in time opens eyes...
a stitch in time celebrates lives...

We will not forget!

(10/16/89)

STATION/BREAK

Break.
Break down
Break up
Break in
Break out
Break even
Break ground
Break loose
Break habits
Break through
Break barriers
Break records
Break free
Break.

(10/21/89)

WAITING GAME

(For Chekesha)

The light is in the window
same as always

waiting for you
beckoning you to home
to warmth
to safety

The light is in the window
where my heart is
where you should be—
secure.

The light is always
in the window
same as ever...
some things never change.

(10/21/89)

BE LOVED

(For TB)

I wrote poems for you:
Tears, joy, pleasure in the brew,
And you never knew.

(7/26/90)

SAX APPEAL

Sultry, sexy, sassy sounds
Take me where I long to be
Arms outstretched...
dancin'...
free.

(7/28/90)

THE PROMISED LAND #3

The view is not so pretty here
the air is not so sweet
that you can fail to hear the cries
that echo down our street.

The grass is not as green as thought
the pathway, strewn with rocks
the rights that blood and sweat had bought
retreat behind new locks.

Unfinished business yet remains
from struggles of the past
for those who feel racism's pain
the chasm is still vast.

We've only breached the "promised land";
we're standing on its shore
we have to go to work again
so things won't be like before.

(7/28/90)

WAKE-UP CALL

Wake me before you go
don't leave me sleeping
wrapped in the
afterglow of your love—
unaware.

Make sure my eyes are open
and that I'm wide awake
before you slip away.

I'll miss you more if I awake
and find that you've gone
without a word
a smile
a kiss
some good-bye token
I could keep.

Wake me before you go
let me close the door
let my sleepy smile
be your invitation
to hurry back.

(8/6/90)

PLAIN SIGHT

(For TB, from Kansas City)

"Look at me."
you said.
I opened my eyes:
saw you
dancing with me
asked you
unuttered questions
felt you
closer than close.

"Look at me."
you said.
I looked at you
smiled
frowned
it's so much easier
to do this dance
with my eyes closed,
my secrets kept.

"Look at me."
you said.
I can see you in the dark—
my partner in this dance;
I feel your lips
your hands
your face.
My open eyes
might tell truths
show fears
confusion.

I look at you
watching me

seeing me
exposed
seeing me,
seeing me—
I close my eyes.

Dance with me
I'll let you see me
dance with me
I'll look at you
dance with me
hold me
dance with me again
look at me
I'll look at you—
eyes open.

(8/24/90)

IT TAKES ALL KINDS

(For all my sisters at BIG, Kansas City)

Rainbow colored
red bright
glistening gold
midnight black
tempting tan
mocha brown...

it takes all kinds.

Hair
short/long
frizzy, straight
Afro'd
permed
braided
jherri'd
dreaded...

it takes all kinds.

Rail thin
short/tall
buxom
skinny
big hips
long legs
big behinds...

it takes all kinds.

Sisters,
we represent
the spectrum
of what's possible...

aren't we beautiful?

Big-nosed
freckled
gap-toothed
almond-eyed
full-lipped
round-faced...

aren't we beautiful?

Smart/silly
sweet/sassy
sexy/sultry
serious/sincere...

we are beautiful!

Head-wrapped
gold-chained
long-robed
short-skirted
kente-draped
dressed to the nines...

it takes all kinds.

Mellow/strong
smooth/light
young/old
dry/sweet
like fine wines...

Sisters, we are all kinds!!

(8/25/90)

TERMINAL ILLNESS

When I am truly dead
that is,
when my lungs
no longer breathe
my eyes
no longer see
blood no longer flows,
a dying process
that began years ago
will be completed.

I have been dying
slowly
painfully
from being out of touch.

I have been dying for years
subsisting on
a semi-starvation diet
of no touch.

How I have survived
this long
is a mystery...
probably due more
to stubbornness
than strength.

(11/11/90)

MAKING THE GRADE

I hope I pass...
I heard this class was hard
the teacher's s'pozed to be a bitch
I hear she gives assignments
the first day of school
I hope I pass this class.

I hear the exams are murder:
and she don't do reviews—
and hardly ever gives make-up tests;
she drops pop quizzes
and she don't grade on the curve
I hope I pass this class.

You should see the book!
's got umpteen hundred pages
we're s'pozed to get through
the whole thing by the end of the term;
a whole bunch'a people
have flunked this course big-time!

Some kids don't do their homework—
she'll call on you anyway
but if you do your work and study
passing's pretty easy.

I heard this class was hard
but lots'a people make it
I'm still sorta new
I got a lot to learn yet

I hope I pass this class!

(12/5/90)

BUILDING BLOCKS/STEPPING STONES

(For Chekesha's Graduation, June 5, 1991)

On this very special day,
I probably won't have time to say
These things; so I wrote them down
For you, for when I'm not around.
You know how much there is to win
So now, as your life you begin:
Don't build your castles in the air;
There's no firm foundation there.
Don't keep your head high in the clouds
Just keep it up above the crowds.
When things seem really hard to do,
Your strong, firm roots will nurture you.
If you feel lost, don't ever fear:
you will always find me near.
Don't worry if you sometimes slip;
Get up, dust off, resume your trip.
Try to keep your thinking straight
as today you celebrate
The start of your road to success,
I wish you nothing but the best!

                Love,

                       Mom

(1/12/91)

A PARENT'S PRAYER

God
help me to live with my limitations;
I am doing the best I can right now.

Help me to live with uncertainty
and to accept things I can't control.
Help to refrain from instantly
blaming myself
when my child does things that are
hurtful or embarrassing
especially if
I've done all the right things.

Help me to keep from bombarding
my child with the "when I was your age" lecture:
these times are not like mine.

Help me to be supportive
when other parents/friends are
having a difficult time:
mine may be just around the corner.

When I hear of a teenager going wrong
Keep me from blaming the parents;
I wish I could personally apologize
to all of those who I previously faulted
for their childrens' delinquencies.

Give me the wisdom to not fight
worthless battles:
bedroom floors and un-made beds
are not serious in the scheme of things:
I have learned to live with closed doors.

Help me understand that teenagers today
don't accept "because I said so"

as an absolute and want reasons
and explanations;
I must re-write my parenting book
frequently,
For this is a whole new world.

Help me keep focused on what really matters:
love, faith, support, and understanding.
If I have these, I can weather anything
that comes my way.

(1/12/91)

HOLDING PATTERNS

Sometimes
the things that we love hurt.

They have thorns
and stickerbriars,
bad odors and
bad tastes.

But we hold on
anyway
savoring the pleasure,
ignoring the pain
(sometimes it's only temporary).

We all have to learn
when to hold tight
and when to let go.

(4/16/91, Phoenix, Arizona)

TEMPORARY IN-SAD-ITY

I was sad today
for no special reason.
Melancholy
crept up on me
and rained out my sunny day.

Seems like
sad saves itself up
and strikes when least expected
like a sudden thunderstorm
on a clear summer day.

I was saddened unexpectedly,
in the midst of a cloudless day—
like a punch in the stomach,
sad deflated my happy mood.

Seems like
sad saves itself up
and must be exorcised
periodically.

(4/19/91, Phoenix, Arizona)

MEMORY LAPSE (UNGUARDED MOMENTS #2)

Just for a while
I forgot
how tenuous our hold
on happiness is.
Life is an
"iffy" proposition
and dreams
are shattered everyday.

It's so easy
to block out
the bad times,
to bury them under layers
of practiced optimism,
smiling at the world;
occasionally forgetting
the pain of times past.

Just for a minute
I thought things had changed:
a temporary memory lapse...
I must remember to be on guard.

4/28/91

BEYOND CONTROL

I keep me
under
lock and key
a controlled substance;
I'm unpredictable
when unleashed.

I should wear
caution/warning labels
to let folks know up front
that what I've got is potent
and can be dangerous.

I mete me out sparingly
in small doses at a time—
I can be hard to handle.

I keep me
under
lock and key
a controlled substance...

let me out!!!!!

5/20/91

SITTING THIS ONE OUT

The steps are familiar
the melody well-known
don't play that song for me,
it brings back memories...
even with unrhythmic feet
I learned to do this dance...

I think I'll sit this one out.

(7/2/91)

WOMAN STRENGTH

Sisters, I submit to you
that like the ad,
our strengths are legendary.

We have the eyes
that though blinded by
torrents of tears,
manage to see better days.

We have the mouths
that defend, define,
defy, and delight.

We have the backs
that form bridges
to brighter tomorrows.

We have the arms
that bear burdens,
reach out, and hold tight.

We heal and recover
from broken bodies
and broken promises.

We nurture children
with little money
little time,
and little help.

We possess the power to hope
in the face of
impossibilities;

We persevere despite
loneliness, lovelessness,
and lunacy.

We have the spirit and the sass
to stare bullshit in the face
and go toe-to-toe
with trouble.

Sisters, I submit to you that
our strengths aren't legendary...
our strengths are f/actual.

(7/19/91)

A MEASURE OF TIME

No clocks help me
to mark the time
of the hours and minutes
marching past.

No calendars
add up the days,
the months, the years,
of cycles
beginning and ending:
I measure time by scars.

The bruises and cuts
of childhood
are trivial
compared to the
wounds of womanhood.

Past events are remembered
by the pain they cost,
the scars left behind;
scabs are the healing signs
of life moving forward.

I look at myself
inside and out
and see a life
lived hard but well.

I run my mind and fingers
over the tell-tale marks
and see a history
of my life's happenings.

Calendars and clocks
don't mark time for me:
I measure time by scars.

(7/20/91)

CLOSED DOORS/OPEN WINDOWS

Darkness...
light.
Despair...
hope.
An endless cycle
of highs and lows—
all part of our life journeys.

All mountains have valleys;
Each apex, a nadir;
Each time a door closes,
a window opens
if we can only see.

Crests...
canyons.
Tears...
laughter.
For every missed opportunity,
new chances arise;
For every mile passed,
a new vista appears.

Darkness...
light.
Sadness...
joy.
Closed doors,
open windows.

Life always goes on.

(11/25/91)

Though no one
can go back
and make a
brand new
START

My friend,
anyone can start
from now and
make a
brand new
END.

Author unknown

PROSE

"LETTING GO"

(Sermon delivered at All Souls Unitarian Church, Washington, D.C., on Sunday, October 28, 1990, for the "Celebration of Women" service.)

MEDITATION

The meditation for July 27th reads: "Who we are and the way we do things is good enough for today. Who we were and the way we did things yesterday was good enough for that day. Ease up on ourselves. Let go. Stop trying so hard. Today, I will let go. I will stop trying to control everything. I will stop trying to make myself be and do better and I will let myself be."[1]

The meditation from October 25th reads: "We can embrace our history, with its pain, its imperfections, its mistakes, even its tragedies. It is uniquely ours; it was intended just for us. Today, we are right where we need to be. Our present circumstances are exactly as they need to be—for now. Today, I will let go of my guilt and fear about my past and present circumstances. I will trust that where I have been and where I am now are right for me."[2]

May we prepare ourselves for worship. Lord, may we learn today that letting go does not mean surrendering, that letting go means growing, that letting go is a part of life.

SERMON

When I was asked to deliver the sermon today, I really didn't have to think hard about what I wanted to talk about and I didn't have to think very long about it, either: the topic of "letting go" sort of whacked me on the top of the head. Now, I don't know if you'd consider that "divine inspiration", but I think it was. As women, we spend much of our lives letting go of things. Indeed, for men and women letting go of things is a natural and recurring part of life.

We let go of our mothers' wombs in tears, pain, and blood to make our way from our first home into a new world: we move from an old to a new place. We let go of our parents' hands to take our first unsteady, unaided steps to begin charting our own directions in life. We let go of our parents' homes to go out on our own and make our own places in the world. For those of us who have embraced Unitarianism as our way of life, we've probably let go of other religious beliefs, dogmas, and traditions in order to be here. And finally, inevitably, sometimes prepared, and sometimes, unexpectedly, we let go of life and we die. Letting go is a part of life.

The difficulty that many of us—particularly women—face, is knowing when to let go. We tend to hold on to things far longer than we ought to, even when letting go is in our own best interest: some things should not be kept. But letting go is hard.

As children, we learned very early and fairly easily about letting go. Some things we learned to let go of quickly, such as sharp objects and hot pans, because they were painful. But as adults, we seem to have lost that ability. We hold onto things, to situations, and yes—even people—when they are emotionally and physically painful to us. We're afraid to let go, to be on our own, to move to a new place.

Letting go does not mean failure or surrender, or giving up—

it means recognizing facts and accepting realities. Clint Eastwood—who would be surprised to hear his name mentioned in a church—when he was playing the cop "Dirty Harry", once said: "A good man must know his limitations." A good woman has to know hers, too! Letting go means facing reality and not denying it.

Knowing one's limitations means letting go of that denial. Another quote from *The Language of Letting Go*, which is a book of daily meditations and I highly recommend it, says: "Denial means we [don't] let ourselves face reality, usually because facing that particular reality would hurt....Denial is a protective device, a shock absorber for the soul. It prevents us from acknowledging reality until we feel prepared to cope with that particular reality."[3] The poet Ovid has said that: "We are slow to believe that which if believed, would hurt our feelings."[4] There is even a prayer for serenity which goes, "God, grant me the serenity to accept the things I can't change, the courage to change the things I can, and the wisdom to know the difference."

We probably all need to let go of circumstances in our lives, and we may be finding it hard to do. Examples may include women who cling to painful relationships or who continually satisfy the needs and wants of others while denying their own. Changing ourselves and our lives is a challenge. Some advice on how to begin that process can be found in Harriett Lerner's book, which is entitled *The Dance of Anger—A Woman's Guide to Changing the Patterns of Intimate Relationships*. Chapter Nine is entitled: "Tasks for the Daring and The Courageous." She says: "Choose a courageous act—make a plan to do something that is not in keeping with your usual pattern."[5] She advises us to break out of our circular dances of repeated, non-productive patterns, to define ourselves, to move slowly and think small (since every journey starts with a single step), to prepare for resistance, and lastly, always, to question things.[6] Letting go can be both daring and courageous!

This whole subject of letting go has been of particular importance to me during the last two years, as I had to cope with an unexpected family crisis. Today seems an appropriate time to say that without the help of friends, many of whom are my fellow All Souls members, I would not have survived intact and I want to publicly acknowledge the prayers, the advice, and the comfort they gave me. I learned that I was not alone in handling my problems and didn't have to solve everything by myself. I was also advised that I needed to learn to let go. As a result of that advice, I let go of more things than I would have ever imagined, and am better for having done so.

A major step in my life-long journey of letting go started when I was 18. I went to the Washington Hospital Center's nursing school. I will be the first to admit that I was rotten at giving shots, and on my first real patient (the oranges, the grapefruits, and the other students we practiced on weren't real), the needle stuck and bent when I put it in the patient's arm. It wasn't my fault, but that's another story.

I survived my first and only autopsy, at least until the pathologists were preparing to saw open the head to examine the brain. I learned that holding people's hands, reading to them, and saying comforting words didn't work for me like it always did for the nurses on Ben Casey and Dr. Kildare. I left nursing school after a year: I had to let go of a long-held dream of a nursing career. For a long time, I felt like I had failed. Sometimes we have to let go of old dreams in order to make way for new ones.

While sitting in a beauty parlor several years ago, I picked up a magazine with an article entitled "Letting Go of Friends." I thought that was a callous notion at the time, but I read the article anyway. It focused on recognizing when friendships were no longer reciprocal and cutting them loose. I couldn't imagine ever doing such a thing! But a while later, while updating my telephone book and my list of special dates, I realized that there were people on those lists who never called me and who never returned my phone calls, whom I continually invited to events but who never came (or never responded), to whom I sent cards and letters but who never wrote back.

Some of these people were people I had known for half my life and who were important parts of who I was. I took the article's advice: I decided to let them go. And though I miss them, I am no longer pained that I don't hear from them. How many of us are still holding on to non-responsive people, afraid to let go?

Many of us like to be in charge of things, especially ourselves. But I've had to realize the limits of my self-sufficiency. I've had to get rid of the notion that I could do everything. (Hold up "Superwoman" shirt.) And literally, two years ago, I folded up my "Superwoman" shirt and put it in the drawer. I don't wear it that much anymore. I know that I don't have to solve my problems by myself anymore, and I've learned to ask for help when I need it. That old song, "I Get By With a Little Help From My Friends", has become my national anthem.

We all have to search our lives to see where we might be holding onto something desperately—or someone desperately—that we need to let go of. Women tend to cling tenaciously to things and people, and ideas that we hold dear. The whole notion of letting go seems sometimes antithetical to our entire nature. We like connected-ness and continuity, even when it's not beneficial. We hang on because we're afraid of change and we frequently stick to what's known because it's either comfortably—or uncomfortably—predictable.

We must let go of people who are toxic to us. We have to learn new ways of co-existing with them that are not hurtful to us. Frequently, these people are our family members. We have to accept that finding a life that works for us may mean letting go of people who have been, and who are important parts of our lives. And in doing this, we also have to let go of the guilt of letting go of them. Again from *The Language of Letting Go:* "Our freedom starts when we stop denying other peoples' issues and politely, but assertively, hand their stuff back to them—where it belongs—and deal with our own issues."[7]

We've been socialized in this country to feel guilty, inadequate, or dysfunctional if our families are not of the "Father Knows Best" or Ozzie and Harriet" variety. We need to let go of our stereotypes about family life and define "family" in a way that works for us. My friends are my family.

We need to continue to let go of ideas about what constitutes "appropriate" roles for men and women that might limit what human beings can be. We need to let go of "requirements lists" (and we all had them or still have them) that define in terms of physical or financial characteristics, what types of people are acceptable to us for love, friendship, and companionship. We need to let go of "nevers" and be open to "possibilities." We have to open ourselves up to new ideas by re-defining our limits and changing our parameters.

We need to let go of the need to be liked by everyone—it's not possible. Women particularly are affected by this insidious affliction. We have to let go of being nice, of sucking things in, and holding our emotions back. We need to cry, scream, holler, or throw tantrums when we find it necessary. We tend to cry inwardly, silently, in corners of dark rooms. Those of us who have suffered bitter life blows are frequently complimented on "how well we hold up", denying our emotions the life-saving healing of release. Giving vent to pent-up, held-back feelings allows us to deal with them, get them out of the way, and move on. Unless we acknowledge and let loose our feelings, they remain with us as unfinished business that doesn't go away. One more thing on our already over-loaded mental and emotional plates.

We have to let go of negative feelings and insecurities and low self-esteem. I'd like you now, if you will, to practice a favorite exercise of mine: raise your right hand, put it over your left shoulder and pat yourself several times and say: "I think I'm wonderful!" Okay, let's hear it! If you're feeling especially good about yourself, say: "I know I'm wonderful!" Okay? Letting go means being honest with yourself about your needs and your feelings and your wants, and bolstering your own self-esteem, letting go of the notion that someone else can do that for you.

We have to let go of the idea that we can always help people. We can't—we're finite and our powers are limited. This is hard, especially for those of us in the helping professions, to accept. We must learn to offer help and to let people know we'll be there when they come to us. People change when they're ready, and not according to our time clocks.

We have to let go of some of our notions about time, especially old time frames that didn't work out the way we'd hoped. What we didn't accomplish by 21, 25, 30, or 40 may not now be worth doing or mourning over. Though we should always plan for the future, we should never forget the importance of the now, and to be happy today. And many of our time frames were artificial and arbitrary anyway.

It may seem as if I'm telling you to let go of everything, but I'm really not. In our lives, there are many good and valuable parts. We simply must become more selective about the parts we keep and the parts we let go of. And today, on a day on which the disciples of racism march in our city,[8] we must let go of hate—because it's destructive, draining, and averts us from other purposes.

Letting go can be gentle and gradual or it may be dramatic and abrupt. There's no directions that come with the process; it's a day by day effort. I'd like to end with the December 4th meditation from *The Language of Letting Go:*

"'How much do we need to let go of?' a friend asked one day. 'I'm not certain, I replied, 'but maybe everything.' Letting go is a spiritual, emotional, mental, and physical process, a sometimes mysterious metaphysical process of releasing to God and the Universe that which we are cling to so tightly.

We let go of our grasp on people, outcomes, ideas, feelings, wants, needs, desires—everything. We let go of trying to control our progress in recovery. Yes, it's important to acknowledge and accept what we want and what we want to happen. But it's equally important to follow through by letting go.

Letting go is the action part of faith. It is a behavior that gives God and the Universe permission to send us what we're meant to have.

Letting go means we acknowledge that hanging on so tightly isn't helping us to solve the problem, change the person, or get the outcome we desire. It isn't helping us. In fact, we learn that hanging on often blocks us from getting what we want and need. Who are we to say that things aren't happening exactly as they need to happen?

There is magic in letting go. Sometimes we get what we want soon after we let go. Sometimes it takes longer. Sometimes the specific outcome we desire doesn't happen. Something better does.

Letting go sets us free and connects us to our Source. Letting go creates the optimum environment for the best possible outcomes and solutions.

Today, I will let go of that which is upsetting me the most. I will trust that by letting go, I have started the wheels in motion for things to work out in the best possible way."

BENEDICTION

(Ecclesiastes 3: 1-8)

To everything there is a season, and a time to every purpose under the heavens:

a time to be born, and a time to die:
a time to plant and a time to pluck up that which is planted
a time to kill and a time to heal
a time to break down and a time to build up
a time to weep, and a time to laugh
a time to mourn and a time to dance
a time to cast away stones and a time to gather stones together
a time to embrace and a time to refrain from embracing
a time to rend and a time to sew
a time to keep silence and a time to speak
a time to love and a time to hate,
a time of war and a time of peace.

And there is a time to hold fast
and a time to let go.

ENDNOTES

1 Beattie, Melody. *The Language of Letting Go* (Daily Meditations for Codependents. San Francisco: Harper and Row Publishers, 1990, p. 211.
2 *Ibid.*, pp. 310-11.
3 *Ibid.*, p. 56.
4 *Ibid.*
5 Lerner, Harriett. *The Dance of Anger—A Woman's Guide to Changing the Patterns of Intimate Relationships.* New York: Harper and Row Publishers, 1985, pp. 194-5.
6 *Ibid.*, pp. 195-6, 198, 217.
7 Beattie, p. 5.
8 The Ku Klux Klan marched in Washington, D.C. on October 28, 1990.

Steppin' over the Glass